A LITTLE BOOK OF DRUGS

by the same author

A Little Book of Alcohol
Activities to Explore Alcohol Issues with Young People
2nd edition
ISBN 978 1 84905 303 7
eISBN 978 0 85700 628 8

A Little Book of Tobacco
Activities to Explore Smoking Issues with Young People
ISBN 978 1 84905 305 1
eISBN 978 0 85700 630 1

Games and Activities for Exploring Feelings
Giving Children the Confidence to Navigate Emotions and Friendships
ISBN 978 1 84905 222 1
eISBN 978 0 85700 459 8

101 Things to Do on the Street
Games and Resources for Detached, Outreach and Street-Based Youth Work
2nd edition
ISBN 978 1 84905 187 3
eISBN 978 0 85700 419 2

Let's Talk Relationships
Activities for Exploring Love, Sex, Friendship and Family with Young People
2nd edition
ISBN 978 1 84905 136 1
eISBN 978 0 85700 340 9

Cyberbullying
Activities to Help Children and Teens to Stay Safe in a Texting, Twittering, Social Networking World
ISBN 978 1 84905 105 7
eISBN 978 0 85700 228 0

Working with Young Men
Activities for Exploring Personal, Social and Emotional Issues
2nd edition
ISBN 978 1 84905 101 9
eISBN 9780857002822

Working with Young Women
Activities for Exploring Personal, Social and Emotional Issues
2nd edition
ISBN 978 1 84905 095 1
eISBN 978 0 85700 372 0

A LITTLE BOOK OF DRUGS

ACTIVITIES TO EXPLORE DRUG ISSUES WITH YOUNG PEOPLE

Second edition

Vanessa Rogers

Jessica Kingsley *Publishers*
London and Philadelphia

First published in 2006 by the National Youth Agency
Second edition published in 2012 by
Jessica Kingsley Publishers
116 Pentonville Road
London N1 9JB, UK
and
400 Market Street, Suite 400
Philadelphia, PA 19106, USA

www.jkp.com

Library of Congress Cataloging in Publication Data
Rogers, Vanessa.
A little book of drugs : activities to explore drug issues with young people / Vanessa Rogers. -- 2nd ed.
p. cm.
ISBN 978-1-84905-304-4 (alk. paper)
1. Youth--Drug use. I. Title.
HV5824.Y68R683 2012
613.8--dc23
2011051698

British Library Cataloguing in Publication Data
A CIP catalogue record for this book is available from the British Library

ISBN 978 1 84905 304 4
eISBN 978 0 85700 629 5

Printed and bound in Great Britain

CONTENTS

ACKNOWLEDGEMENTS

I would like to thank:

Dave Price (A-DASH), Chrysalis Drugs Project, Hertfordshire Young People's Substance Misuse Team, Gillian Porter (Hertfordshire PCT), Deborah Mulroney (HCC School Improvement and Development Service), Joshua, Toby and Sophie Oakes-Rogers (Simon Balle School).

Thanks also to my team and any other youth workers not mentioned who have been a part of the projects mentioned.

ABOUT THE AUTHOR

Vanessa Rogers is a qualified teacher and youth worker with a master's degree in Community Education. She has over ten years' experience within the Hertfordshire Youth Service both at practitioner and management levels. Prior to achieving national recognition for her work Vanessa managed a wide range of services for young people, including a large youth centre and targeted detached projects for Hertfordshire County Council. She now devises and delivers professional development training and writes for *Youth Work Now*. In addition she has been commissioned to devise training packs for a wide range of organizations, including the BBC.

This book is one of 20 practical resources written by Vanessa to support the development of creative youth work and social education.

Her website www.vanessarogers.co.uk gives detailed information about further titles, training and consultancy visits.

INTRODUCTION

Most young people will come into contact with drugs, including tobacco or alcohol, at some stage in their life and will need to make decisions and choices. This includes 'hard to reach' young people, who need innovative ways of engaging them, and those with disabilities who may be additionally vulnerable.

This book offers creative ways to engage young people in activities and discussions that explore values and attitudes, develop skills to make informed choices and give information to learn about legal and illegal substances. It deliberately does not include alcohol and tobacco, which are the subject of the companion books to this resource, *A Little Book of Alcohol* and *A Little Book of Tobacco*, also available from Jessica Kingsley *Publishers*.

The aim of drug awareness work is to give information and support that enables all young people to develop the skills to help them towards making positive choices and keeping safe. Therefore, drugs awareness sessions must be relevant to the lives of young people, reflecting their own knowledge and experiences of drugs, both positive and negative. Simply telling them not to do it or trying to frighten them with horrific stories intended to scare will rarely work. For example, if a young person's experience is completely different from the one reported in the newspaper, they are likely not only to disregard that information but become distrustful of other official information sources too.

Instead, information must be credible, factually correct and presented in a non-judgemental way that encourages young people to question their existing knowledge and values, and think through the possible consequences of actions and choices. This includes giving information about health risks, the legal status of drugs and the consequences of illegal drug use.

This resource is a diverse collection of activities suitable for work with young people aged 13–19 to look at drug-related issues, including prescription drugs, over-the-counter medicines, herbal remedies and legal highs, as well as those that are illegal. It is divided into three sections: Warm-ups, Activities and Review Tips. Each session plan can be used as a 'stand-alone' activity or put together with others to build a comprehensive curriculum over a few weeks.

Warm-ups

This section offers short activities and exercises to open a session around drugs or to re-energize a group after a discussion. Easy to use, these are ideas to introduce issues and enable facilitators to begin to assess the level of knowledge and attitudes to drugs within the group.

Activities

Including ideas for group and individual work, these activities look at three main areas:

- Information and knowledge about drug issues.

- Exploring attitudes and values, including peer influence and reducing risk.
- Developing skills to make healthy choices.

Review tips

The final pages suggest a few ideas for reviewing and reinforcing learning. It is important to allow time at the end of a session for these as they help evaluate the effectiveness of sessions and inform your needs analysis for further work.

GROUND RULES

Any sessions intended to educate young people about drugs and illegal substances require a degree of sensitivity about the extent to which the young people are familiar with the subject. As well as health risks and the social issues that can arise from addiction, there are clear laws in place which make the buying and selling of illegal substances a criminal offence.

To accommodate the different abilities, levels of knowledge, understanding and experience within any group it is important to create a safe learning environment that sets clear boundaries and explains confidentiality from the start. Often called 'ground rules' or a 'group contract', these principles can be referred back to as the sessions progress, providing a familiar framework for working safely and respectfully together.

Make it clear before you start that there is no assumption that all young people will take or have taken drugs. However, do stress that if they disclose something that is illegal, or potentially harmful to themselves or others, then you may need to share that to keep within professional confidentiality boundaries. This could include telling their social worker, notifying the police or reporting your concerns as a child protection issue. Whatever your decision, please ensure that you record all conversations thoroughly and discuss your concerns with your line manager, in line with your organization's policies. One rule that I often suggest for inclusion is that no one should ask or be asked personal questions. The aim of this is not to stifle confidences, but to enable young people to relax safe in the knowledge that embarrassing questions will not be fired at them.

The other thing to consider is that despite the legal status, many young people will know someone who has experimented with drugs, and some will have family members who use them too. 'Drugs' are a taboo subject at home for many young people for a variety of reasons including faith, culture and fear. However, other young people might be living with a family member with drug dependency issues or a drug-related criminal record.

Equally, as the topic can be extremely contentious make sure that the need to respect each others' points of view and experiences is fully considered.

DRUG INFORMATION

Drug classifications

The term 'drug' is used to describe many legal and illegal substances, including tobacco and alcohol. It also includes volatile substance abuse (VSA), for example, of lighter fuel, glue or aerosols. To help define the differences, drugs are often classified into three groups by the effect they have on the body. These are 'depressants' (e.g. heroin and tranquillizers), which have a sedative effect that slows down the way the body and brain function; 'stimulants' (e.g. cocaine and amphetamines) that give a false burst of energy and the illusion of being more alert; and finally 'hallucinogens' (e.g. magic mushrooms and LSD) that can alter the way someone feels, sees, hears, tastes or smells.

Some drugs, such as alcohol (a depressant), fit neatly into one category. Others, such as ketamine, cross categories as they can have more than one effect.

Illegal drugs and health risks

As well as being given information about the immediate and possible long-term health effects of substance misuse, it is vital that young people understand that the effects of drugs can be unpredictable. Not all drugs are the same and different drugs have different dangers and risk factors associated with them.

Unlike prescribed medication and drugs bought from a pharmacy, street drugs do not come with a label on the side to tell you what is in them, and the effects can vary from person to person. This is not just dependent on the purity of the drug but also on the strength of the dose, whether it is mixed with other drugs, where the young person is when they take the drug, who they are with and most importantly how they are feeling. These are sometimes referred to as the 'drug, set and setting' factors.

Thc potential dangers of drug use will also depend on:

- *Quantity*. Taking large quantities of any drug increases the potential dangers and risk of overdose. For example, consuming large amounts of a stimulant drug such as cocaine can result in panic attacks, aggression and chest pains that present similar to a heart attack. Large quantities of a hallucinogenic drug (e.g. magic mushrooms) may lead to frightening and disturbing experiences. Smoking large quantities of cannabis could increase the risk of poor mental health and create lethargy. A high dose of any drug, including legal ones, can lead to a loss of control, unsteady movements, raised blood pressure and poor decision-making, consequently increasing the likelihood of accidents or of doing something that is regretted later.
- *Frequency*. The more often a drug is taken, the greater the health risks, particularly if the body is not given time to recover in between doses. With some drugs a tolerance can develop, meaning that more needs to be taken in order to get an effect.
- *Combining*. Taking drugs together purposely or by mistake can produce unpredictable and sometimes dangerous effects. For example, alcohol can be very dangerous mixed with opiate-based painkillers.

- *How*. Intravenous drug use is potentially the most dangerous way to take a drug. This is because of the additional risks of contracting infections such as HIV or hepatitis if needles are shared, alongside the general risks associated with the drug itself.

Prescription drugs

Prescription drugs can only be prescribed by a doctor (or qualified health care professional) and dispensed by a pharmacist. Before prescribing, the doctor will assess the patient, looking at all of their medical history and checking for allergies, to make sure that the drugs are safe and will treat whatever ailment the patient has. Even then most medicines come with a leaflet to explain possible side-effects and what to do should you be affected.

So prescription drugs are usually very safe to take, as long as the doctor's instructions are followed and the recommended dosage is taken. However, prescription drugs can be misused to get a 'high', or taken with alcohol to increase the effects, making them potentially as dangerous as illegal drugs.

Like illegal substances, prescription drugs are sometimes sold on the street, or online. The problem here is that no matter how good the website is, or how many times the person selling assures you that it is the 'genuine article', you can never really be sure about what you're getting. Even if it is the real thing, when taken excessively prescription drugs can have similar negative side-effects to illegal drugs. It is also illegal to have possession of a controlled substance without a prescription, so young people should be clear about this and not take medication prescribed for someone else.

The message to young people is to only take drugs that have been prescribed for them by a professional and not to share their medicines, even if someone has the same symptoms.

Over-the-counter drugs

Any drug education curriculum should include exploring the potential dangers of misusing over-the-counter (OTC) medicines. This is a multi-million pound industry that includes painkillers, vitamins, cough medicines and thousands of other medicines that can be found in the bathroom cabinet and first aid boxes of most households.

Over-the-counter medicine refers to those that can be bought without a prescription. However, some drugs, for example, codeine and aspirin, can be prescribed as well as sold in small quantities. Many young people (and adults) think that because a drug is available to buy in a pharmacy or supermarket it cannot be as strong or as dangerous as other substances. This is not necessarily true as many of the drugs that can be bought in a drug store are simply lower doses of those available on prescription only.

OTC medications can be deliberately misused by mixing them with alcohol, doubling or trebling doses to maximize effect, extracting the active ingredients, crushing tablets to snort or preparing with water to inject. However, people who do not realize the dangers inherent in taking more than the recommended dose or going over the daily dosage can unintentionally misuse OTC drugs. This is particularly true of paracetamol, used for pain relief and to reduce temperatures. While generally safe for use at recommended doses it can cause fatal liver damage in extreme cases, particularly if mixed with alcohol.

To avoid overdose or becoming dependent it is important always to follow the instructions given, including looking for any warnings about what to avoid whilst taking the drug. You should also always tell your pharmacist if you are taking any other medication, even cough sweets, before purchasing anything.

Herbal remedies

Herbal medicine, also called botanical medicine, refers to using a plant's seeds, berries, roots, leaves, bark or flowers for medicinal purposes. Despite advances in medicine, homemade syrups, teas and tinctures, or buying patented remedies from health food stores, remain popular.

From the earliest times to the present day, people have used herbs to treat a wide range of ailments. These are often passed down through generations, becoming a trusted family remedy for anything from headaches to period pains.

Since the 1990s, herbal medicine has become much more mainstream, with many doctors and medical practitioners supporting herbal treatment alongside traditional prescription-only drugs. This is because massive advances in technology mean that herbal medicines can now be scientifically analysed, quality control standards can be set in place and clinical research can demonstrate the effects. Alongside this, many patients like the idea of using 'natural' medicines and place high value on them.

However, just because these products are 'natural' doesn't mean that there are no dangers involved. Many of them include ingredients that are used in prescription medicines that can cause adverse reactions when used with other drugs (including alcohol). For that reason it is important that doctors or pharmacists are aware of what is being taken so they can advise on whether to continue herbal treatments alongside any prescribed drugs.

Legal highs

Often sold at music festivals, in specialist shops and online, legal highs are substances used like illegal drugs such as cocaine or cannabis, but are not covered by current misuse of drugs laws, and so are legal to possess or to use.

However, they are still normally considered illegal to sell under medicines legislation and some later become illegal to possess or sell; for example, mephedrone (Meow Meow). Some drugs marketed as legal highs actually contain ingredients that are illegal to possess. Others are sold as 'research chemicals' or plant food and labelled as 'not for human consumption' to get around the law. So, although they are marketed as 'legal' this may not be strictly true and could leave people unwittingly breaking the law.

Although these drugs are sold as legal substances they are not subject to the same rigorous tests as legal drugs and medicines, which sometimes take years of testing between conception and actually being available. This means that legal highs are not necessarily safety approved for use, and in some cases may carry serious health risks. This is because the chemicals they contain may never have been intended for human consumption, so have not been tested to show that they are safe.

Finally, as with any drug that has not been prescribed or bought in a drug store, users can never be certain what they are taking and what the effects might be.

UK and Northern Ireland – Misuse of Drugs Act (1971)

In the UK there are two main statutes that regulate the sale and availability of drugs, the Misuse of Drugs Act and the Medicines Act. Other drugs, for example, alcohol and tobacco, are controlled with laws that state the age you need to reach before being allowed to buy them.

The Misuse of Drugs Act (1971) divides drugs into three classifications, A, B and C. These are broadly based on their harmfulness either to the user or to society when they are misused, and are the subject of many debates between politicians and health experts. Class A drugs are considered the most harmful, so they have the most severe penalty for possession and supply. Drugs controlled under the Misuse of Drugs Act are illegal to have, produce, give away or sell. This includes young people putting their money together and giving it to one person to buy the drugs. The fact that it was intended for all of them will not be taken into account if the young person gets caught, and he or she could be charged with trafficking, or 'supply' as well as possession.

Class A

These include cocaine and crack (a form of cocaine), ecstasy, heroin (diamorphine), LSD, methadone and magic mushrooms.

MAXIMUM PENALTIES

- Possession – seven years and/or an unlimited fine.
- Production/trafficking – life and/or an unlimited fine.

Class B

These include cannabis (including skunk), codeine, amphetamines and barbiturates.

MAXIMUM PENALTIES

- Possession – five years and/or a fine.
- Production/trafficking – 14 years and/or an unlimited fine.

Class C

These include GHB, ketamine, Rohypnol and minor tranquillizers.

MAXIMUM PENALTIES

- Possession – two years and/or a fine.
- Production/trafficking – 14 years and/or an unlimited fine.

Just because a drug isn't illegal doesn't mean that it cannot cause harm. Currently there are many discussions in the media about the status of 'legal highs', developed to mimic the effects of illegal drugs such as cocaine and ecstasy, but structurally different enough to avoid being classified as illegal substances under the Misuse of Drugs Act. However, they can still have dangerous side-effects and over time might well be added to the list of drugs regulated by law.

Offences under the Misuse of Drugs Act

These can include:

- possession of a controlled drug
- possession with intent to supply another person

- production, cultivation or manufacture of a controlled drug
- supplying another person with a controlled drug
- offering to supply another person with a controlled drug
- import or export of a controlled drug
- allowing premises you occupy or manage to be used for the consumption of certain controlled drugs or supply or production of any controlled drug.

USA – Controlled Substances Act (1970)

The 1970 Controlled Substances Act provides the legal framework for the prevention of drugs misuse in the USA. It consolidated many existing laws regulating the manufacture and distribution of a wide range of illegal drugs, or 'narcotics', as well as prohibiting the chemicals used in the production of controlled substances (http://nationalsubstanceabuseindex.org).

Schedule I

(a) The drug or other substance has a high potential for abuse.

(b) The drug or other substance has no currently accepted medical use in treatment in the United States.

(c) There is a lack of accepted safety for use of the drug or other substance under medical supervision.

Schedule II

(a) The drug or other substance has a high potential for abuse.

(b) The drug or other substance has a currently accepted medical use in treatment in the United States or a currently accepted medical use with severe restrictions.

(c) Abuse of the drug or other substances may lead to severe psychological or physical dependence.

Schedule III

(a) The drug or other substance has a potential for abuse less than the drugs or other substances in schedules II and I.

(b) The drug or other substance has a currently accepted medical use in treatment in the United States.

(c) Abuse of the drug or other substance may lead to moderate or low physical dependence or high psychological dependence.

Schedule IV

(a) The drug or other substance has a low potential for abuse relative to the drugs or other substances in schedule III.

(b) The drug or other substance has a currently accepted medical use in treatment in the United States.

(c) Abuse of the drug or other substance may lead to limited physical dependence or psychological dependence relative to the drugs or other substances in schedule III.

Schedule V

(a) The drug or other substance has a low potential for abuse relative to the drugs or other substances in schedule IV.

(b) The drug or other substance has a currently accepted medical use in treatment in the United States.

(c) Abuse of the drug or other substance may lead to limited physical dependence or psychological dependence relative to the drugs or other substances in schedule IV.

Involving parents and carers

Many parents and carers feel very uncomfortable discussing drug and alcohol issues with their children. Often this is because they have little knowledge themselves, apart from what they see in the media, and feel that what they do know about drugs is outdated and therefore not useful. Some are also scared that their son or daughter may be using drugs and decide either to ignore it or to get angry and demand answers.

To help empower parents to have open and frank conversations, as well as reassuring them and increasing their confidence about drugs, consider sending home a drugs information leaflet with a website address to find out more. Alternatively, you could support the young people to host a drugs awareness session for their parents and other adults in the community.

Parents also need to be clear about organizational drug policies and know what will happen if a young person is involved in a drug-related incident; for example, smoking in a non-smoking area, or possession or selling of illegal substances. This is particularly important where a youth worker is going to be loco parentis; for example, on an overnight trip away from home. Information given should include legal requirements, including the need to pass safeguarding information on, and any exclusion processes that may be enforced, including the right to appeal.

WARM-UPS

DEFINITIONS

This is a whole-group warm-up activity that encourages young people to share their understanding and knowledge.

Aim

To reinforce the wide range of substances meant by the term 'drugs', both legal and illegal.

You will need

- Flipchart
- Markers

How to do it

Start off by asking the group to idea-storm as many names of drugs as they can think of. Stress that you are not asking how many they have taken or seen, just heard of.

Record them onto flipchart paper as the young people call them out.

Next ask the young people to split into groups of three or four. Their challenge is to come up with a definition of what a 'drug' is. They can illustrate this if they want to – the point is to discuss the term and reach agreement.

Once everyone has finished, invite each group to share what they have been working on.

Finally, offer this definition:

> A substance people take to change the way they feel, think or behave.
>
> (United Nations Office on Drugs and Crime 2012)

What do the young people think of this? Explain that this is a definition that many schools, youth services and other professionals work to.

Display the young people's definitions on the wall to refer to in future sessions.

STEREOTYPES

This activity explores stereotypes and is good to use as a warm-up with small groups of young people.

Aim

To raise awareness of stereotyping and encourage further discussions.

You will need

- Flipchart paper
- Plenty of coloured markers
- Sticky tack

How to do it

Hand each young person a piece of flipchart paper and some markers. Explain that you are going to call something out and you want them to draw the first things that come into their head. Emphasize that this is not a drawing competition and that they can use any style that they like.

When everyone is settled with pen poised, say, 'DRUG DEALER!'

Give the group ten minutes to draw, encouraging them to think about age, gender and ethnicity as well as clothes and hairstyles. Ask that they do this without looking at each others' sheets for the moment.

At the end of the time ask everyone to stop. Invite each young person to show their picture to the rest of the group, explaining any particular bits they want to draw attention to before sticking it on the wall. Encourage the group to discuss how they decided what to draw and what influenced their choices.

Invite the young people to ask questions of each other about what they have drawn and encourage questions and discussion.

Pull out the main themes emerging from the pictures and record them on another sheet of paper. Facilitate a group discussion about any stereotypes emerging. How true are these? Ask the young people to think about their own experiences or knowledge and compare this.

Finally suggest that most drug dealers do not fit the stereotype of a man in a coat and dark glasses waiting at the school gate. It is far more likely to be someone they know or an older sibling of someone they know who approaches them. Would this make it easier or harder to say no?

DRUG CHAIR SWAP

This activity can easily be adapted for young people with mobility issues or wheelchair users by facilitating it seated in one chair throughout. Instead of moving they can simply raise a hand to show the sticker.

Aim

This game is based on the well-known party game 'Musical Chairs' and is a fast-paced way to assess knowledge in the group and give facts in a fun way.

You will need

- Chairs (one less than the number of people playing)
- Stickers
- Marker pens

How to do it

Prepare stickers by labelling them C, E, A or H (to stand for Cannabis, Ecstasy, Alcohol and Heroin). You will need a sticker for each player, and if possible four equal sub-groups.

Introduce the session by showing the young people the labels and explaining what the letters stand for. Hand each young person a sticker, to be stuck onto their back where it is visible. Seat everyone in a circle, all except one person who should remain in the middle.

Explain that you are going to read a list of facts that apply to one or more of the drugs. Every time the young people hear a fact that can be applied to the drug their letter represents, they should stand up. Once standing they should swap chairs with another standing person as quickly as possible. Point out that some facts are specific to one drug, but others are true for several. For example, only heroin is sometimes called 'horse', so for that round only those with a letter 'H' on their back should move. However, it is illegal to possess heroin, cannabis and ecstasy in any form so for that round everyone with a letter 'H', 'C' or 'E' should compete for seats.

As there are not enough chairs, one person will be left without a chair each time. As a forfeit for not grabbing a chair they should offer another fact or comment about the drug on their sticker. They then start the following round in the centre of the circle, ready to try to secure a seat in the next applicable round.

Stress that the idea is to learn more about different drugs and there is no expectation that everyone will know all of the answers. Correct any wrong answers and leave space for questions and discussion between rounds.

STATEMENTS

1. You are sometimes called 'horse'. (Heroin)
2. You are a depressant drug. (Alcohol and Heroin)
3. A street name for you is 'blow' or 'grass'. (Cannabis)
4. You are a powerful painkiller. (Heroin)
5. You are often smoked using a 'bong'. (Cannabis)
6. You are often injected. (Heroin)
7. You usually come in pill form. (Ecstasy)
8. You are usually drunk in liquid form. (Alcohol)
9. You often make people hungry after using you. (Cannabis)
10. There is a specified age to legally buy you. (Alcohol)
11. The most important psychoactive ingredients in you are tetrahydrocannabinols – THC. (Cannabis)
12. You are often smoked with tobacco. (Cannabis)
13. You are sometimes called a 'dance drug'. (Ecstasy)
14. You are legally available to buy in lots of places. (Alcohol)

15. You are usually measured in units. (Alcohol)
16. The chemical name for the pure form of you is 3,4-methylenedioxymethamphetamine or MDMA for short. (Ecstasy)
17. A street name for you is smack. (Heroin)
18. You are illegal to possess in any form at any age. (Heroin, Cannabis, Ecstasy)
19. You are often served in a glass. (Alcohol)
20. You are sometimes cut with ketamine. (Ecstasy)

DRUG PAIRS

This is a good way to divide the group into pairs before starting the main activity.

Aim

To introduce the session topic and provide opportunities for the group to interact.

You will need

- A set of the 'Drug cards 1'
- A few spare cards in case you have too many young people and have to improvise

How to do it

Shuffle the cards and ask each young person to choose one. If you have an odd number in the group use a blank to make up another card along one of the themes, for example 'ECSTASY', 'PILLS' or 'E's'.

Invite everyone to look at their card, but ask them not to tell anybody else what is written on it. It does not matter if you have duplicate 'pairs', so long as each person can find a partner.

Ask the group to find their pair. They can only do this by asking questions about the drug on their card; for example, they cannot ask, 'Have you got a card with another name for ecstasy on it?' but could ask, 'Are you a dance drug?'

'Drug cards 1'

CANNABIS	**LSD**	**COCAINE**
GRASS	**ACID**	**COKE**
SOLVENTS	**CRACK**	**GLUE**

ROCK	ECSTASY	HEROIN
TOBACCO	AMPHETAMINE	MEPHEDRONE
PILLS	SMACK	FAGS

SPEED	MEOW MEOW	

DESCRIBE IT!

This is an exercise to demonstrate the importance of effective listening in communication.

Aim

To guess your partner's drug card from the information they give you.

You will need

- Copies of the 'Drug cards 2' (you will need a card for each young person)

How to do it

Divide the group in half. One half will be 'A's' for this activity and the other 'B's'. Ask the B's to find an A to work with so that they are in pairs. Next ask each pair to take two chairs, place them back to back and then sit down so that they are facing away from each other.

Hand all the A's a drug card, and ask them not to show their partner, explaining that the 'B's' task in this first round is to listen as carefully as possible to the information that will be given to them. The A's should then proceed to describe the drug on their card as carefully and in as much detail as possible, giving all the information that they know or have heard about it. The only rule is that they cannot actually say the name!

After about two minutes call time and invite the B's to guess what was on the card. Collect in and shuffle before handing out to the B's for another round.

Review the exercise – what made it easy to know what was on the card? What made it hard? What information was the most useful?

'Drug cards 2'

CANNABIS	TOBACCO	COCAINE
ECSTASY	HEROIN	CRACK

SKUNK	LSD	AMPHETAMINES
STEROIDS	CAFFEINE	ALCOHOL

I HEARD

This is a small-group activity that explores myths and stereotypes based on information that young people may have heard about drugs.

Aim

To promote discussion and explore young people's knowledge.

You will need

- A copy of the 'I Heard' sheet for each young person, cut up into strips
- An envelope for each set
- Pens
- A box

How to do it

Hand each young person an envelope containing a set of the 'I Heard' slips and a pen. Ask them to quickly complete the sentence on each piece of paper. Encourage them to go with their first thoughts rather than deliberating too long.

When they have completed all their slips collect them all in the box. Make sure you shake the box well so that all the statements become muddled up.

Now ask the young people to sit in a circle and pass the box around the circle. Each young person should take a slip and read it out. For each one ask them if they think the statement is true and where they think the ideas came from. Once the person who has read it out has spoken, encourage comments from the rest of the group.

Reinforce correct information and facilitate a discussion around stereotypes and values regarding drugs information.

'I Heard' sheet

All drugs are…	Using cannabis leads to…
People take drugs because…	All drug addicts are…
Legal highs are…	Drug dealers are…
If you try drugs you will…	If the police catch you with drugs they will…

DRUGS WORDSEARCH

This warm-up uses a format that most young people will know so it requires little explanation!

Aim

To open up discussions about drugs and substance misuse, encouraging young people to work together.

You will need

- Copies of the wordsearch enlarged to A3 size
- Coloured felt pens
- Prize (optional)

How to do it

Divide the young people into groups of three and hand each group an A3 copy of the wordsearch and a coloured felt pen.

Explain that the task is to complete the wordsearch as quickly as possible. First group finished wins!

Review the activity, making sure that the young people are clear about the meaning of terms used and explaining if they aren't.

Drugs wordsearch

C	W	D	V	J	U	E	N	I	A	C	O	C	O
A	S	O	L	V	E	Y	J	M	S	S	A	L	L
N	O	I	T	P	I	R	C	S	E	R	P	A	M
N	L	E	E	I	D	F	T	P	C	O	O	S	J
A	V	S	G	L	J	K	M	S	S	X	A	S	G
B	E	Q	A	L	H	E	E	T	T	K	V	I	S
I	N	D	E	P	R	E	S	S	A	N	T	F	M
S	T	R	V	G	E	R	T	R	S	U	K	I	O
A	S	U	G	Y	U	R	I	Y	Y	K	V	C	K
I	S	G	Q	A	A	M	M	U	O	S	C	A	E
N	C	B	U	N	J	K	U	I	I	T	S	T	W
J	W	T	L	A	G	E	L	L	I	R	E	I	A
E	S	J	A	G	E	R	A	L	V	E	T	O	N
C	D	B	L	O	O	E	N	R	D	E	G	N	J
T	B	L	O	O	D	S	T	R	E	A	M	F	B
H	A	L	L	U	C	I	N	O	G	E	N	I	C

Search to find the following substance-related words:

Cannabis
Stimulant
Classification
Depressant
Prescription
Bloodstream
Hallucinogenic
Solvents
Skunk
Pill
Smoke
Inject
Illegal
Ecstasy
Drug
Cocaine

SCRAMBLED WORDS

This activity is another one that will be familiar to young people so should need little explanation.

Aim

To help assess young people's knowledge of common drug names.

You will need

- Copies of the 'Scrambled Words' sheet
- Pens

How to do it

Ask the young people to choose a partner to work with.

Hand out a copy of the 'Scrambled Words' sheet to each couple and a pen. Explain that the task is to unscramble the words, using the clues to help them, as fast as they can.

First pair to complete the sheet wins! Go through the sheet, ensuring that everyone understands the names and terms used.

'Scrambled Words' sheet

OCEINCA – A white powder derived from the coca plant =

EITAHEMANPM – A stimulant drug =

PNIRISA – A well known painkiller =

SCIBANAN – This substance is usually smoked =

IROHNE – A painkilling drug made from the opium poppy =

ETSSLNOV – These substances are inhaled =

MTEEAKNI – An anaesthetic drug legally produced for use with humans and animals =

COTOACB – This contains the stimulant drug nicotine =

RPEPPSO – A term for amyl, butyl or isobutyl nitrates =

SSYETAC – The chemical name for this is methylenedioxymethamphetamine or MDMA =

DRUGS QUIZ

Quizzes are a great way to start a session as they are quick and usually good fun. You can use this one either with a group, as described, or with individual young people.

Aim

To assess the knowledge in the group and to open up discussion.

You will need

- A small piece of red and green card for each participant

How to do it

Hand each participant a red and a green card. Explain that you are going to read out some statements about drugs and alcohol.

Once you have read each statement the young people should hold up a green card if they think the statement is true, and a red one if they think it is false. If they are not sure then they will need to hold up both cards. So that this doesn't become just an easy option and an opportunity not to really participate, explain that whilst it is fine to vote 'not sure', you will be asking people why they are not sure and facilitating discussions.

Take the opportunity to stress that you are not asking who has used any (or all) of the substances mentioned and that it is not a problem if they do not know the answer. Stress that it is impossible to know everything about drugs – it is more important to know where to get information from if needed.

Answer any questions raised, or show the young people where to access the information, and use the level of correct answers within the group to inform your needs analysis for future workshops.

DRUG QUIZ QUESTIONS

1. Alcohol is a stimulant drug.

   False. Alcohol is a depressant.

2. 'Skunk' is a very strong type of cannabis.

   True. It contains much higher levels of tetrahydrocannabinols (THC), the important psychoactive constituent of cannabis.

3. The most dangerous way to take any drug is by injecting it.

   True. Injecting drugs carries many risks, as most of the body's natural defences are bypassed. The most widely recognized risks are the transmission of blood-borne viruses such as hepatitis B and C and HIV through sharing needles, syringes and injecting paraphernalia. However, there are numerous other health risks associated with injecting.

4. Stimulants such as mephedrone and cocaine give you extra energy.

   False. Stimulants do not give you extra energy – it just feels that way! What happens is that they increase existing energy reserves and make you feel like you have more, but afterwards they can leave users feeling tired and depressed.

5. Tobacco smoking causes far more deaths per year than all illegal drugs put together.

   True. There are estimated to be around 120,000 smoking-related deaths per year – far more than associated with illegal drugs.

6. The recommended safe drinking limit for women is 5 units a day.

   False. Safe drinking limits are 2–3 units a day for women and 3–4 for men. This is for adults over the age of 18: there is no safe drinking level for under 18's.

7. Some young people who use cannabis will eventually end up using 'hard' drugs.

   True. But the vast majority won't.

8. Using legal highs available at music festivals or on the internet is safe because they are made from natural ingredients.

   False. There is no safety guarantee for any substances bought in this way because they are not tested or regulated, making it hard to be 100 per cent sure what is actually in them. Being labelled 'natural' does not mean that a substance cannot have an adverse effect or react badly to other chemicals in the body, including alcohol. Many 'legal highs' are under review and new legislation may be put in place to change the legal status in the future.

9. It is illegal to sell solvents such as glue and gas to under 18-year-olds.

   True. In the UK it is an offence 'if she/he (meaning the shopkeeper) knows or has reasonable cause to believe that the substance or its fumes are likely to be inhaled for the purpose of intoxication'.

10. All wild mushrooms make you hallucinate.

    False. The most common magic mushroom in the UK is the 'liberty cap', and the other more potent type is the 'fly agaric'. Eating the wrong kind can be very dangerous, causing sickness, diarrhoea and even in extreme cases of poison, death.

DRUGS IN SPORTS

This is a quick warm-up to open up discussion around drugs in sports. It works well with the activities in the next section.

Aim

To quickly assess opinion in the group and get an understanding of existing knowledge.

You will need

- A red, yellow and green card for each person

How to do it

Give each young person a red, a yellow and a green card. Explain that you are going to read a series of statements and you want the young people to raise the card that corresponds with their opinion:

RED = No, I disagree!

YELLOW = I want to say something about this.

GREEN = Yes, I agree!

Allow time for people to ask questions or make comments about the statements. If no one uses a yellow card you can ask questions or challenge red and green cards.

Highlight group agreement and facilitate discussions with care where people feel the most differently.

DRUGS IN SPORTS STATEMENTS

1. Random drugs tests are the only way to stop athletes cheating.
2. Drugs in sports have been a problem since the 1980s.
3. Athletes caught using steroids should be barred for life from competing.
4. Disabled athletes should be subject to the same rules as other athletes otherwise it isn't fair.
5. If someone refuses a drugs test then he/she must have something to hide.
6. It would be better if every sportsperson was drugs tested before competing.
7. I think sportspeople provide good role models for young people.

8. If a sportsperson is found to have used drugs before winning a medal then it should be taken from them.
9. Athletes who are wrongly convicted should be given their titles back and apologized to.
10. It is acceptable for athletes to use performance-enhancing drugs to help them be the best they can.

WORD SCATTER

This is a group warm-up activity that could be adapted to explore personal values.

Aim

To look at language and attitudes associated with substance use/misuse.

You will need

- Post-it notes
- Large sheets of paper
- Felt tip pens

How to do it

Divide the young people into groups of four. Hand out a small wad of Post-it notes and a pen to each young person and a large sheet of paper to each group. Working in their groups, invite each young person to think of as many words or thoughts that come into their head when they hear the term ‘substance misuse’, write them on a Post-it note and stick it onto their group sheet. If you think the group will be unfamiliar with this term exchange it for ‘drug user’. At this stage all contributions are welcomed and not challenged.

After five minutes call time and ask each group to display their sheet to share with everyone. Often the list of words will include a number of slang words or emotive terms that may be considered offensive; for example druggy, smack head, addict.

Explore with the group some of these terms and the possible effects they might have upon our behaviour. Where do we get our information? Is it true of all people who misuse substances? Does it differ for legal and illegal drugs?

ACTIVITIES

CHALLENGING THE STEREOTYPES

Aim

To consider stereotypes and assumptions about drug use/misuse.

You will need

- Flipchart paper
- Markers
- Sticky tack
- Eight pieces of card labelled: cannabis smoker, alcoholic, crack smoker, ecstasy user, solvent user, heroin user, cocaine user, person who does not use drugs

How to do it

Divide into small groups and allocate one card to each. Ask each group to draw what they think a person using the drug on the card looks like.

Stick the drawings on a wall and then ask the young people to guess from each others' drawings which drug the person uses. Next, ask how they made these decisions, what information or knowledge it was based on and if their assumption was correct.

Introduce the idea of stereotypes. Discuss what it means and offer the following definition:

> A stereotype might be defined as a generalization and assumption that together portrays the reputation of a group.

Now, facilitate a discussion that considers:

1. Are the drawings based on stereotypes?
2. How are gender, age and ethnicity represented in the drawings?
3. Where do people get information about drugs and drug users? (Introduce the role of the media here if it hasn't been mentioned.)
4. Can you tell who might use/not use different drugs just by looking at them? If so, how?
5. What can happen if incorrect assumptions are made about people?

Finally, invite the young people to share their own experiences of being stereotyped and conclude that you cannot always tell if a person is using or misusing drugs just by their appearance, the music they like or the friends they have.

DRUG RISK CONTINUUM

This is a whole-group activity to explore risk-taking behaviour in relation to drugs and substance misuse.

Aim

To assess potential risks, and promote discussion about keeping safe.

You will need

- A set of 'Drug Risk' cards
- Two A4 sheets labelled 'VERY RISKY' and 'NOT VERY RISKY'

How to do it

Ask the young people to sit in a seated circle and hand each a 'Drug Risk' card, asking them not to share what is on their card.

Place one of the A4 sheets on one side of the circle where everyone can see it and the other on the opposite side.

In turn invite each person to read out what is on their card, and then place it where they think it should go between the two poles. Encourage them to explain their decision but stress that you are not asking if they have done it, just their opinion.

Set a rule that at this stage only the person who has the card can speak or make the decision.

Go around the circle until all the cards have been used and then ask if anyone wants to move a card. If so, they must explain why they want to move it.

Once all the cards are in place, facilitate a discussion about the situations described on the cards. Explain that the effects of some risky behaviour are immediate; for example, solvent abuse can cause a swift death, whilst others may not become obvious for years; for example, lung cancer caused through smoking tobacco.

Reinforce the need to think through all of the risks before making decisions that can have an impact on all areas of your current and future life.

'Drug Risk' cards

Taking more than the recommended dose of aspirin to cure a headache	Regularly drinking three times the recommended weekly units for safe drinking	Having unprotected sex whilst drunk
Smoking skunk every day	Snorting cocaine on a night out so you can carry on drinking alcohol	Using amphetamines to stay awake to revise for an important test

Walking home at night alone after taking MDMA	Going to a remote place to 'trip' on LSD	Smoking cannabis as part of your faith or culture
Buying herbal sleeping pills from a health food shop	Ordering diet pills from the internet	Drinking red wine as part of a religious ceremony

Smoking to suppress your appetite	Growing your own cannabis	Sitting in a confined space whilst a friend is smoking
Using someone else's prescribed medicine as you have the same symptoms	Taking cocaine to feel confident	Making tea with magic mushrooms

Misusing solvents	Drinking bottles of cough medicine to get high	Driving after smoking skunk
Buying legal highs at a music festival	Binge-drinking alcohol at weekends	Using ecstasy at parties

Using sedatives to come down after taking stimulant drugs	Lying to get prescribed more painkillers after an injury has healed	Stealing Ritalin to use as a stimulant

MAKING DECISIONS

Aim

To explore how decisions are made and how other people can impact on this, both positively and negatively.

You will need

- Paper and pens
- Flipchart paper

How to do it

Set the scene by asking the young people to tell you the last decision they made. Record ideas and conclude that we make decisions all day long, from what to wear and whether to have tea or coffee through to more important decisions; for example, whilst driving or crossing the road.

Move on to ask the group, 'How do we make decisions?' Note any feedback on a flipchart sheet and offer ideas if necessary; for example, tossing a coin, consulting the stars, asking a friend, looking online or asking someone else to choose for you.

Next, explain that you are going to read out a list of drugs (write them on the flipchart if you think that is more appropriate) and ask some questions, followed by a series of tasks relating to it.

DRUG LIST

- Cannabis
- Heroin
- LSD
- Tobacco
- Alcohol
- Ecstasy

QUESTIONS

1. Which drug is the most harmful?
2. Which drug is the least harmful?

TASKS

Task 1

Each person should make an individual decision about the questions.

Task 2

Ask the young people to choose a partner to work with. They should compare answers, explaining how they reached a decision. If they have different answers then they should discuss them and try to reach agreement.

Task 3

Divide the main group into groups of six, keeping the pairs together. Read through the drug list again and repeat the questions. As a group they should discuss the drugs and then rank them all again, this time in a continuum of harm from the most through to the least.

Invite each group to share their decisions and explain the reasons behind them. Facilitate a discussion to consider the importance and value of knowing how to make effective decisions. Point out that to make a properly informed decision about the questions asked the term 'harmful' should have been explained. For example, did the question mean the drug most harmful to individual health, the impact on society or harmful in terms of the legal consequences? Conclude that it is hard to make good decisions without having all the information.

Discuss strategies that the young people may find helpful in similar situations. For example, find out more about the drug, ask the opinion of a trusted friend, consider the financial/social consequences of any decision made, consider health implications. Stress the importance of taking advice and listening to people but having confidence in your own decisions to stand up for yourself, even if that means going against the majority decision.

HOW I LEARN

This can be used as a group activity or scaled down for one-to-one work.

Aim

This is an activity to assess young people's learning styles and preferred ways of receiving information.

You will need

- Five pieces of flipchart paper
- Sticky tack
- Pictures (optional)
- Five different colour packs of Post-it notes

How to do it

In advance take the pieces of flipchart paper and label them 'LOOKING ON THE INTERNET', 'TALKING WITH FRIENDS', 'LISTENING TO A PRESENTATION', 'READING LEAFLETS' and 'ROLE-PLAY AND GAMES'. To make these more visual, either draw simple pictures, for example, a laptop on the 'INTERNET' sheet, or cut out photos from magazines to stick on.

Divide up the Post-it notes to give each young person a small wad with one of each colour in it. Choose a different colour to represent the numbers 1 to 5.

Start the activity by suggesting that people learn in different ways. Some people are visual learners; for example, they like watching films or looking at diagrams. Others like to hear things, enjoying discussions or learning through music, and some prefer to learn through role-play or games. It can be useful to know your own preference because it helps you choose learning opportunities that suit you.

This includes information about drugs and alcohol, which is available from a wide range of sources. Go on to suggest that not all of this is reliable, and that it can be difficult to know where to go for information that is accurate as well as interesting. Ask the young people where they currently get information from and encourage discussion about the reliability of their sources.

Next, stick the posters with the five different ways of obtaining information up around the wall and hand each young person a stack of sticky notes.

Explain that each colour sticky note represents a number 1 to 5. Their task is to look at the different ways of finding out information about drugs shown on the posters, and then stick the sticky note representing the number 1 on their first choice.

Repeat the exercise in order of preference until they have used all the notes.

Review the results and discuss with the group the top choices, asking the reasons why they like this method of learning best.

You now have a needs analysis from which you can devise further sessions to suit the young people's learning styles.

DRUGS – PROBLEMS AND BENEFITS

Aim

To reinforce that not all drugs are 'bad' and look at the positive use of drugs and medicines as well as the negative.

You will need

- Flipchart paper
- Markers

How to do it

Split the young people into small groups and hand each group flipchart paper and markers. Divide the flipchart sheet into two columns, 'PROBLEMS' and 'BENEFITS'.

Explain that you want each young person in turn to suggest a 'problem' that they think drugs can bring and a 'benefit' that they think drugs can have. For example, a negative is that if you buy illegal drugs you cannot know exactly what is in them; a benefit of some drugs, such as insulin, prescribed for people with diabetes, is that they are vital for maintaining that person's health. All suggestions should be noted down under the appropriate heading.

Invite each group to share a point from their list for discussion, encouraging other groups to ask questions or reinforce what has been suggested. Take the opportunity to challenge any incorrect statements or explore stereotypes.

Reflect on the findings, reinforcing the important role that prescribed and some over-the-counter drugs have played in the fight against disease and illness. Conclude that it is often how drugs, including legal medicines, are misused that makes them dangerous, rather than the drugs themselves.

ACCEPTABLE/UNACCEPTABLE

The idea of this activity is to get young people to think about their own values and those of their peers.

Aim

To open up a discussion around personal values.

You will need

- A set of the cards depicting situations
- A card marked 'ACCEPTABLE' and a card marked 'UNACCEPTABLE'

How to do it

Hand each young person a situation card and ask them to read it, but not show anyone else.

Mark two opposing poles on the floor with the 'ACCEPTABLE' and 'UNACCEPTABLE' cards. Explain that what you want the young people to do is to 'rate' the cards as acceptable or unacceptable behaviour. Stress that there is not always a right or wrong answer, although there are legal implications for some choices. Some responses are based on cultural or social acceptance, which may differ within the group.

For each card, agreement needs to be reached within the group before it is placed in a zone. If there are different views, facilitate a discussion ensuring that everyone is heard and more assertive members of the group do not take over.

When all the cards are placed down, review the process. How easy was it to reach consensus? Was it easy to listen to views that opposed their own? What influenced their decisions?

'Acceptable'/'Unacceptable' cards

Giving a friend a painkiller if they have a headache	An athlete taking steroids to improve their performance
A man ordering Viagra from the internet to improve his sexual performance	Putting a substance in someone's drink without them knowing
Taking sleeping tablets prescribed for someone else	Smoking cannabis to help relax

Buying cigarettes for someone under 18	Driving a car after drinking alcohol
Clubbing together with friends to buy a gram of cocaine before a party	Calling someone 'mad' because they are prescribed anti-depressive drugs
Putting pressure on someone to have sex when they are drunk	Excusing aggressive behaviour by saying that it was caused by too much cocaine

Being unable to remember what happened the night before after mixing strong prescribed painkillers with alcohol	Not getting up for school the morning after smoking skunk
Buying someone a double shot of spirits when they asked for a single	Selling solvents to younger people who you suspect may misuse them
Reassuring a friend who regularly smokes cannabis because they are feeling paranoid and anxious	Calling a friend's parents because they are unconscious after drinking a bottle of spirits

WHAT HAPPENS NEXT?

This is shown as a small-group activity but if you have a very small group give each young person a scenario to work with.

Aim

To encourage young people to think through possible consequences of substance-related situations.

You will need

- A flipchart sheet for each group
- Pens
- 'What Happens Next' scenarios

How to do it

Divide the large group into smaller groups of three or four. Hand each group a different scenario, explaining that each depicts a situation where drugs or alcohol is an issue.

Give each group a flipchart sheet and markers and ask them to construct a comic strip to show what happens next. Encourage the groups to think about the consequences of actions, what they may have done differently in the situation and what could be done to resolve the scenario.

'What Happens Next' scenarios

A 14-year-old boy is caught at school with cannabis in his school bag
A 21-year-old young man offers an 'E' to a 15-year-old girl he has just met in a club
A 17-year-old girl passes out at a club after drinking a bottle of vodka
A 16-year-old student tells her tutor that she uses cannabis to relax her

DRUGS JENGA

This activity uses a well-known game and adapts it to look at drugs issues. The fact that the questions are random means that it is possible to discuss attitudes and knowledge, and assess skills, in a non-personal way.

Aim

To remove wooden bricks from the Jenga tower and answer questions.

You will need

- One wooden Jenga game (a Milton Bradley game) on which you have written the drugs questions
- Black permanent marker pen
- A flat, level surface

How to do it

TO CREATE THE GAME

Using a black permanent marker, write on a selection of Jenga blocks the name of a drug, or a question about drugs from the list on the next page. You can add your own to personalize the set.

Build the Jenga blocks into a high tower, including those with questions and drug names on, placed so that the writing cannot be seen.

TO PLAY THE GAME

Each player in turn should attempt to remove one block from the stack of Jenga blocks, without knocking the whole thing over.

If the chosen block has a question on, the young person should read it out loud, before answering it (if they can) and then replacing the block at the top of the tower. If they get the answer wrong, or cannot answer it, they must take another block and try again.

If they pull out a block with the name of a drug written on it, they should tell the group three things they know about it, and then put the block on top of the pile.

If a blank block is pulled, then the player only has to place it onto the top of the tower.

If a player wants to miss a question, they can put the block on top without answering, but must then take another block.

If a block is pulled that has already been answered, then the young person must also place it on top and then pull another one.

If a player knocks the tower over, the other players get to choose any of the questions to ask them and after the answer is given the game ends.

Drugs Jenga names and questions

COCAINE	CANNABIS	ECSTASY
SKUNK	MAGIC MUSHROOMS	CRACK
HEROIN	SOLVENTS	LSD
AMPHETAMINE	POPPERS	TRANQUILLIZERS
What are some of the health risks for injecting drugs?	If a friend collapses after using drugs what should you do?	Why do you think it can be dangerous to mix drugs?

What can you do to prevent your drink being 'spiked' in a pub or club?	What class drug is cannabis?	Which common drinks contain the stimulant caffeine?
What are some of the solvents that can be found in most homes?	Why is dehydration a problem for ecstasy users?	What are the dangers of using solvents alone?
Do you think there is a link between drug use and unsafe sex? Why?	Who could you tell if you were worried about a friend's drug use?	What should you do if you find used needles and syringes in a park or playground?
What are the dangers of exceeding the dosage of paracetamol?	Can you name three illegal substances?	Someone offers you a lift home, but you know they have been smoking puff – what do you do?

What is the difference between cocaine and crack?	What would you tell a friend who wants to try ecstasy for the first time?	What is the difference between cannabis and skunk?
What are the names of some commonly prescribed tranquillizers?	What does LSD usually look like?	Do you think most young people try illegal drugs at some point?
What are some of the street names used for cannabis?	What is cocaine often called?	What could you do if someone offered you a drug and you didn't want to try it?

EXPLORING ATTITUDES TO CANNABIS

This is an activity that challenges personal values in a non-confrontational way, encouraging group members to say what they really think.

Aim

To explore young people's attitude to cannabis and the surrounding issues.

You will need

- Information and/or leaflets about cannabis

How to do it

Explain to the group that you are going to read out a series of statements that describe feelings and views about cannabis. You can expand this to include 'skunk', a generic name often used to describe a potent form of cannabis.

The area to the left is the 'agree' zone, to the right is the 'disagree' zone and in the middle is the 'undecided' zone.

Ask the young people to show you how they feel about the statement you read out by moving to the zone which most corresponds to their opinion. Point out that this is not a test, but rather an exercise to find out what the group thinks. Try to encourage the young people to make their own decisions, rather than following their friends' views.

Leave space between statements to review what is being said and make sure that there is an opportunity for questions and to debate issues raised.

Agree with the group any follow-up work or future sessions to take this further.

CANNABIS STATEMENTS

1. Most young people try cannabis.
2. Smoking cannabis leads to trying other drugs.
3. You can always tell if someone has been smoking skunk/cannabis.
4. Celebrities should set a good example to young people and not admit if they smoke cannabis.
5. It is socially acceptable to smoke cannabis.
6. Smoking cannabis is a good way to relax.

7. Cannabis should be available on prescription as a painkiller.
8. The media portray all cannabis users as criminals.
9. Cannabis dealers should get the maximum jail sentence if they are convicted.
10. Some music genres promote smoking cannabis as a good thing.
11. Cannabis should be legalized and taxed by the government.
12. A conviction for cannabis could stop you being considered for some jobs.
13. Most drug users become criminals to pay for their habit.
14. What is safe drug use for one person may not be for another.
15. Smoking helps to keep your weight down.

WHY DO DRUGS?

Aim

To identify key reasons for not taking illegal drugs, and explore why some people might choose to.

You will need

- Two sheets of flipchart, one headed 'DO' and the other headed 'DON'T'
- Marker pens

How to do it

Start the session by asking who drinks tea, coffee or cola, where and how often. Point out that all of these drinks contain a legal stimulant drug called caffeine. Go on to ask if any of the young people know someone who says they can't get out of bed without a cup of tea, or who says they need a coffee in the morning to wake them up. Suggest that this could be the result of a dependence on caffeine, which can be difficult to give up.

Go on to ask which other legal drugs the young people have used, or seen used, in the last six months, encouraging them to call out names. This could include prescription medicines such as antibiotics or over-the-counter cold and flu remedies.

Continue to ask the young people to call out reasons why they think people use these drugs.

Now split the main group into two. Explain that this time you are going to ask them to consider why people choose to take or not take illegal drugs. Hand one group the sheet headed 'DO' and the other the one labelled 'DON'T'. Ask the young people to discuss their ideas in the group and then record them under the heading given.

'Do's could include – peer pressure, to increase confidence, to have a good time, have a new experience, relaxation, depression or ignorance.

'Don't's could include – scared of being out of control, scared of getting caught, cultural values, health concerns, not interested, moral viewpoint or damage to future career aspirations.

Invite each group to present their findings and discuss responses as a whole group. Make sure you consider both the emotional and physical affects of decisions made, as well as the legal standpoint. Conclude that there are lots of reasons why some people choose to use illegal drugs, and lots of reasons for not taking them. Suggest that alongside these, before people make any decisions, they should weigh up the potential benefits and losses too.

LEGAL HIGHS

This session can be facilitated in small groups or with individuals. Before you start, collect some information about legal highs to ensure that all of the young people know what is meant by the term.

Aim

To encourage discussion about legal highs and raise awareness of the health and safety concerns.

You will need

- A set of 'Legal Highs Pyramid' cards for each small group

How to do it

Divide the young people into small groups and give each group a set of the 'Legal Highs Pyramid' cards. Explain that on each card is a reason NOT to experiment with substances marketed as legal highs.

The task for each group is to read the cards, discuss the importance, and then agree a 'pyramid' of reasons why people should avoid using them. The most important reason should be placed at the top, moving down to the concern that the young people think is of least importance. It should end up with four cards along the bottom row, then three, two and finally one at the top.

Allow about 20 minutes for the pyramids to be agreed. When everyone is happy with their cards call time.

Now, review the pyramids. Are they all the same? Where there are differences, ask the groups to share the thinking behind their decision. Facilitate discussion and encourage the young people to challenge decisions, ensuring that this does not become an opportunity for personal attacks on individual values.

Conclude by suggesting that just because a substance is legal, it is not necessarily safe to use. As with other drugs, the risks increase if you combine these substances with alcohol, or other substances.

Point out that most drugs that are now illegal were once freely available. For example, in the First World War families could buy first aid kits containing morphine in syringes to send out to their menfolk on the front, and ecstasy was readily available through marriage guidance centres (similar to today's Relate) for couples going through a rocky patch. As their effects and risks became better understood, they were controlled by legislation. This has already happened to some legal highs and is likely to continue as more becomes known about them.

'Legal Highs Pyramid' cards

You don't know exactly what you are taking	The effects can be very unpredictable
You don't know if you are getting value for money	Some contain substances that are used in plant food or weedkiller
They can cause sickness and diarrhoea	Some contain substances that are illegal
They can contain potentially dangerous chemicals	Most are illegal to sell
Because they are not licensed there have been no safety tests done	The long-term health risks aren't known

BASIC DRUG SORTING GAME

This is an activity for young people with disabilities to give basic information. You can change the cards to illegal substances or introduce new categories, such as cannabis, later on.

Aim

To clarify the level of knowledge in the group and the fact that not all drugs are illegal or 'bad'.

You will need

- A set of 'Basic Drug Sorting Game' cards for each group
- Leaflets and drug information to support the session

How to do it

Point out that not all drugs are illegal. Introduce the idea of legal drugs, some of which are used every day, such as caffeine in drinks, and others found at home in the form of household cleaners, etc. A good way of introducing the topic of medicines is to say that all medicines are drugs, but not all drugs are medicines and discuss who should administer common medicines and the dangers of self-administration. If you are working with young people who regularly use prescribed drugs, then discuss the importance of never giving medicine prescribed for you to anyone else. Check out the young people's knowledge of the terms used.

Divide the large group into smaller groups of five or six. Hand each group a set of cards in an envelope and a sheet of large paper divided into five sections: 'SOLVENTS', 'CAFFEINE', 'MEDICINES', 'ALCOHOL' and 'TOBACCO'.

Allow 15 to 20 minutes for each group to talk about each slip and place it in the correct place. Check out placement and correct if wrong.

Give each group a category to work further on, handing out the leaflets for reference and setting them the task of:

1. naming two other drugs in the same category
2. describing the effect of the drug
3. describing a danger of using the drug.

If this is not appropriate due to the level of understanding in the group, do the first part and then discuss when they might see people using the drug – for example, alcohol at a wedding, or paracetamol if you have a headache. You can then go through the dangers of misusing the drug and techniques for keeping safe.

Ask each group to present their findings to the rest of the young people and then facilitate a question-and-answer session between groups, supplying answers if necessary.

'Basic Drug Sorting Game' cards

AIR FRESHENER	GLUE
MARKER PENS	LIGHTER FUEL
WINE	BEER
GIN	WHISKY

TAILOR-MADE CIGARETTES	**CIGARS**
PIPE TOBACCO	**ROLLUPS**
PARACETAMOL	**COUGH MIXTURE**
ASTHMA INHALER	**INSULIN**

AEROSOL DEODORANT	ALCOPOPS
RITALIN	SLEEPING TABLETS

POSTERS

This is a good activity for larger groups, but it will work if you have a smaller one by asking the young people to work in pairs.

Aim

To develop research skills, spark debate and encourage the young people to question their findings.

You will need

- Flipchart paper
- Glue
- Scissors
- Markers
- A wide selection of leaflets and information sheets about illegal drugs
- Internet access (optional)

How to do it

Divide the main group into smaller groups of four. Put all of the information and leaflets you have collected about different drugs in a place that everyone can see and have easy access to.

Explain that you are going to designate each group the name of an illegal drug and that the group's task is then to research and design a poster to give information to other young people about it. The information should include:

- the legal classification of the drug
- any street names they know
- a description of the substance
- the effects it has on the body.

Explain that they can cut pictures out of the leaflets, get information from the internet and use the markers to create their own images. Reinforce that this is not an anti-drugs poster you are asking them to create, but one that gives good, clear information that would be useful to young people.

Allow 30 to 40 minutes for the posters to be completed and then ask each group to present their poster and findings. Allow time for discussion and encourage questioning. Then review which poster the group thinks is the most effective and why. Put the posters to a show-of-hands vote.

Display the posters for other young people to see.

RISKS AND SKILLS

This group activity offers a scenario to work from. If you think that it is appropriate you can ask young people to work from their own experiences instead.

Aim

To identify risks and personal skills needed to make things safer.

You will need

- Flipchart paper
- Markers

How to do it

Ask the young people to imagine a train journey involving a group of young men and a group of young women coming home late after a night out. Both groups have had a great night out and are loudly laughing and shouting.

At least two of the young women have drunk large amounts of alcohol and are feeling very sick and dizzy. The other young women have also been drinking but they are OK and are looking after their friends.

The young men, who the girls don't know, have been to a club and have all taken ecstasy, except for one young man who is sitting quietly slightly away from the larger group.

There is also an older woman in the carriage travelling alone and two older men seated together.

The young men notice the young women and start calling over to them to get their attention.

Now ask the young people to get into pairs and discuss what they think may happen next and the risks to safety they can identify to everyone involved.

Ask the young people to share in the large group some of their ideas. These could include risks such as one of the girls being sick on the train, arguments breaking out, getting off at the wrong stop or someone getting hurt. Draw out any behaviour that could be linked to the substances taken. For example, the young men, who have used E, may not respect personal boundaries and get too close to the young women.

From the discussions pull out four main risks and write these on four sheets of flipchart paper.

Divide the young people into four groups and hand a 'risk' and some markers to each group to look at. Invite the young people to discuss the risk in their group and then record what could be done to reduce the risk to make it more likely that everyone in the carriage will get home safely.

Once they have done this, ask them to look at the points they have made and think about what personal skills would be needed to be able to do this; for example, assertiveness or thinking ahead and phoning for help.

In the large group, look at the skills identified and facilitate a discussion. How many of the group feel confident that they have these skills? What do they think they would do in similar circumstances?

From this you can plan additional work to build on personal skills.

MEDIA WATCH

This activity can be expanded to looking at other forms of media such as movies or TV.

Aim

To review media articles about drugs misuse and promote discussion about the messages given.

You will need

- A good selection of newspaper/magazine articles
- Copies of the 'Media Watch' sheet
- Pens

How to do it

Ask the young people to look through newspapers/magazines and cut out any articles that feature stories involving drugs. Set a period of about two weeks for them to collect as much as they can, and collect as much as you can too so that there is a wide selection. Try to find the most diverse views that you can!

Divide the main group into smaller groups of four and invite them to share their articles, supplementing these with some you found.

Allow about 20 minutes for discussion, encouraging the young people to record findings onto the 'Media Watch' sheet to share in the larger group later.

Once everyone has finished, invite the groups to share the 'messages' that they picked up on in the articles they read. Facilitate a whole-group discussion to consider the drugs information given in the articles. Are the messages all the same? Which ones should be trusted?

'Media Watch' sheet

What it says	Newspaper/ magazine	Date	What message was being given

DRUGS, ALCOHOL AND THE MEDIA

This activity can be expanded into a wider project that considers all forms of the media and advertising.

Aims

To explore the values and attitudes around drugs and alcohol expressed in the media and prompt discussion.

You will need

- A selection of news stories about drug-related issues
- A selection of adverts for alcohol cut from magazines
- Flipchart paper
- Marker pens

How to do it

Divide the young people into groups and give each a selection of the newspaper articles about drugs. Ask them to read them through and then discuss them, making notes as they go along on the flipchart paper.

Discussion points:

1. What messages do the media give about drugs?
2. Is it the same for all drugs? Are some seen as worse than others?
3. How are the people in the articles portrayed? Does this differ for celebrities and 'normal' people?

Once the discussions are well under way, hand out the magazine adverts for alcohol. Ask the young people to now consider how this 'drug' is portrayed, pointing out that companies are paying lots of money to advertise it and encourage people to buy their product.

Invite each group to feed back on their findings. These should include the availability and acceptability of consuming alcohol and the legal status of drugs such as cannabis and cocaine compared with alcohol.

DRUGS AND MEDICINES

This session considers issues of trust and the effectiveness of different remedies and medicines.

Aims

To raise awareness about over-the-counter and prescription medicines and the dangers of buying online.

You will need

- The list of remedies suggested written onto a sheet of flipchart paper
- Information leaflets

How to do it

Ask the young people about their health and the different kinds of medicine they have taken in their lives. For example, ask what remedies they use or believe cure the common cold. Do they believe the medicine they take will work and be good for them? Explore why, and suggest that over-the-counter and prescribed drugs have been tested to make sure they are safe, have dosage instructions, information about potential side-effects and are clearly labelled to show what is in them.

In pairs, ask the young people to imagine that they feel unwell and have decided to take something to alleviate the symptoms. They should discuss which of the following options they trust to make them feel better and which they don't. Rank them in order of preference:

1. Prescription medicines
2. Over-the-counter medicines
3. Herbal medicines
4. Aromatherapy
5. Hypnosis
6. Acupuncture
7. Surgery
8. Self-medicating (for example using alcohol or cannabis)

Once again point out that whilst many of these are safe if used exactly as instructed by a doctor or pharmacist, some of them, dependent on where you buy them, have not been tested and in effect the user does so at their own risk. Invite the young people to suggest which drugs this might apply to. Point out that one of the major concerns about using illegal or unlicensed substances, aside from the legal consequences, is that users have no real knowledge of what they are taking or of any possible side-effects. This is especially true of drugs such as mephedrone, legal highs or 'diet pills', which can be freely available on the internet.

Point out that many drugs do not mix well with alcohol as they create another chemical in the body, so it is important not to drink if using prescribed, over-the-counter or even illegal drugs.

Stress that prescription drugs should never be shared, even if someone has similar symptoms. Drugs are prescribed specifically, taking into account individual health issues, and some become illegal if possessed without a prescription. Discuss which health conditions might impact on a person's reactions to drugs; for example, asthma, high blood pressure, depression or an underlying heart condition – none of which may be visible or known by either the person sharing their drugs, or the person taking them.

Summarize that if a doctor prescribes a drug they will take all health issues into account, including things such as breastfeeding or existing medications, before deciding which drug is appropriate. Similarly, a pharmacist will ask lots of general health questions before making recommendations. Self-medicating, for whatever reason, does not have this safety net and therefore can be dangerous or cause problems. Invite suggestions as to what these might be. For example, stimulants such as cocaine can result in increased aggression, being drunk can make people more clumsy and increase the risk of accidents, cannabis can make users lethargic and any drug can affect decision-making.

PRESCRIPTION, HERBAL, OTC OR OTHER?

Although this sorting game is shown as a group activity it can be easily adapted to work with individuals.

Aim

To consider prescription, herbal and over-the-counter medicines.

You will need

- A large sheet of paper on which is drawn a circle divided into four. The quarters are labelled 'PRESCRIPTION', 'HERBAL', 'OTC', 'OTHER'.
- A copy of the drugs sheet, cut up.

How to do it

Place the prepared circle in the middle of the group and remind the young people what the terms prescription, OTC and herbal remedies mean. Point out that there is also a section for those drugs that do not fit into any of the other categories.

Give each young person a card and in turn ask each participant to read out what is on it before placing it on the section of the circle that they think is correct. Set a rule that no one else can challenge where it is placed until everyone has had a turn.

Once the circle is complete, ask if anyone wants to move a card and the reason why. Correct any incorrect cards and then review the activity.

Start by pointing out that cannabis is not available on prescription, over the counter or as a herbal remedy. In the UK it is a Class B drug, although some of the components are synthesized for use in other drugs, usually used for arthritis or similar conditions. In this form the THC has been removed so that the 'high' is not experienced.

Review the prescription-only drugs – codeine, Viagra, antibiotics, inhalers, steroids, methadone, sleeping tablets, Ritalin and anti-depressants. These are prescribed by a doctor for an individual and should never be shared, even if the symptoms are similar. Ask the young people to show by a raise of hands how trustworthy they consider the drugs prescribed by a doctor.

Move on to consider the medicines available over the counter – aspirin, paracetamol, flu and cold remedies, vitamin C and cod liver oil. Point out that some prescription drugs, such as codeine, are available in lower doses to buy in a chemist or pharmacy too. Aspirin and paracetamol can also be prescribed, as well as being widely available everywhere from drug stores to gas stations! Other popular buys are vitamin C tablets, although natural remedies for this include eating more fruit, for example oranges and kiwis, and vegetables with high levels of vitamin C in them, to keep healthy.

Again conduct a quick poll to see how much trust the young people place in medicine they can buy over the counter.

Finally, point out that herbal medicine is used to treat many conditions, such as asthma, eczema, premenstrual pains, rheumatoid arthritis, migraine, menopausal symptoms, chronic fatigue and irritable bowel syndrome, among others. A popular herbal remedy is feverfew (a member of the sunflower family), which is a plant that has been used for centuries to reduce fever and treat severe headaches and migraines.

Many of the prescribed drugs included in this activity have an alternative herbal remedy for the same ailment. For example, your doctor can prescribe sleeping tablets, and you can buy herbal remedies over the counter, but you may also want to try putting lavender oil, said to be a natural sedative and sleep inducer, onto your pillow or burn a little in an oil burner before bedtime.

The use of herbs is an ancient approach to strengthening the body and treating disease. Herbs, however, may alter the effects of some prescription and nonprescription medications. Because of this, herbal remedies should be taken with care, preferably under the supervision of a health care provider qualified in the field of botanical medicine.

Once again, facilitate a quick poll to see who trusts the effectiveness of herbal remedies, inviting the young people to share the reasons behind their opinion.

Add up the scores to find out which sources of medicinal remedies the young people trust most. Go on to explore the reasons why, and conclude that it is best to use drugs that are prescribed, or sold on the advice of a pharmacist or qualified herbalist, because you know exactly what you are buying. Make sure that doctors are always made aware of any alternative remedies or over-the-counter drugs being used, just in case they react adversely. This advice includes any illegal substances that young people have been using, such as cannabis or ecstasy, which can have a bad reaction when taken with some prescribed medicines.

'Prescription, Herbal, OTC or Other' drugs sheet

COD LIVER OIL	INHALERS	LAVENDER OIL	GINSENG
STEROIDS	ASPIRIN	METHADONE	ST JOHN'S WORT
CANNABIS	PARACETAMOL	ANTIBIOTICS	FLU AND COLD REMEDIES

RESCUE REMEDY	VIAGRA	ANTI-DEPRESSANTS	SLEEPING TABLETS
FEVERFEW	VITAMIN C	RITALIN	CODEINE

STIMULANT, DEPRESSANT OR HALLUCINOGEN?

Whilst facilitating this activity it is important to stress that the effects of any drug can vary from person to person dependent on where they are, who they are with and how they are feeling.

Aim

To divide drugs into the effects that they are likely to have on someone. It is also worth reinforcing that what might be a safe dose for one person could be dangerous for another.

You will need

- Sets of the 'Drugs Cards' sheet cut up and put into envelopes
- Three A5 cards for each set, marked 'STIMULANTS', 'DEPRESSANTS' and 'HALLUCINOGENS'

How to do it

Start the session by explaining that one way that drugs can be classified is by the effect they have on the body. These are 'Stimulants', 'Depressants' and 'Hallucinogens'. Divide the young people into small groups of four or five.

Hand each group an envelope with the drugs slips inside and a set of the A5 cards. Explain that on the A5 cards are three categories that drugs tend to be split into based on the effects they have on the body.

The group's task is to discuss the drugs on the cards and then place them in the category that they think fits the effect. Allow 10 to 15 minutes and then call time.

Go through the right answers, asking the group to explain where they decided to place their cards and why. Tell the young people to award their group a point for each correct answer.

Go on to point out that some drugs, such as ketamine, actually fit into more than one category. This is because ketamine is a very complex drug, with anaesthetic, analgesic, stimulant and psychedelic properties.

Reinforce what has been said and add up the points. The group with the most is the winner!

Stimulant, depressant or hallucinogen?

STIMULANTS Increase the activity of the central nervous system
DEPRESSANTS Reduce the activity of the central nervous system
HALLUCINOGENS Alter perceptions of reality and may result in hallucinations

'Drug Cards' sheet

STIMULANTS	DEPRESSANTS	HALLUCINOGENS
Caffeine	Alcohol	Magic mushrooms
Tobacco	Solvents	LSD
Methamphetamine	Minor tranquillizers	Cannabis
Amphetamines	Valium	Skunk
Ecstasy	Codeine	

STIMULANTS	DEPRESSANTS
Cocaine	Pethidine
Crack	Heroin
Poppers	DF118 (dihydrocodeine)
Mephedrone	Morphine
	Rohypnol
	Opium

FINDING OUT ABOUT DRUGS

This whole-group activity can be scaled down for effective one-to-one work over several sessions.

Aims

To ensure that if young people are offered something they know what it is. The activity acknowledges that it can be hard to make good decisions without knowing the facts.

You will need

- Six sheets of A3 paper with the titles 'CANNABIS', 'HEROIN', 'COCAINE', 'ECSTASY', 'AMPHETAMINES', 'MEPHEDRONE' (you can vary these to respond to local need)
- Six marker pens (each a different colour)
- Clock
- Drugs information leaflets

How to do it

Divide the young people into six groups and hand each group a different A3 sheet. Explain that they have three minutes to quickly write down all the words and information they know about that drug. Call time and pass the sheets on to the next group. Repeat the process until all six sheets have had a contribution by every team and the groups have the sheet they started with.

Allow time for the groups to see what other young people have added to their original sheet. Invite each team to present the information gathered, suggesting they put a question mark by anything they are not sure of or want to query. Discuss ideas and correct anything that is wrong, stressing that no one can know everything about drugs. In particular, encourage young people to share current alternative or street names used locally for drugs; for example, grass for cannabis or meow meow for mephedrone.

Conclude that the names used for drugs change depending on who is talking about them, the locality and the culture. Ask the young people to suggest why that might be; for example, so that people don't know what they are talking about or to evade the law. Finish by suggesting that it is really important to know what something is, especially if someone is considering taking it or is with people who are using it.

DRUGS IN SPORTS DEBATE

A news story is suggested for this activity. However, it is fine to substitute this for a local or more recent article.

Aim

To promote discussion around decisions made following positive drug testing in sports.

You will need

- Copies of the news story
- Flipchart paper
- Markers

How to do it

Before you start, open the session by explaining that the issue of drugs in sports is not a new one. In the 1960s Tommy Simpson, one of Britain's greatest cyclists, died during the Tour de France after taking a stimulant drug.

Go on to state that drugs are banned in sport to prevent one competitor gaining an unfair advantage over another. However, some athletes continue to take the risk despite knowing the consequences.

Now divide the young people into two groups and hand each group a copy of the news story. Set group one the task of formulating the argument for giving Alain Baxter his medal back. Tell group two that their task is to argue that the decision to strip Alain Baxter of his medal was the right one. Explain that each group will need to present their case to the other. Give out flipchart paper for the young people to record points on.

Allow about 20 minutes for discussion and then set up the room for a debate with group one on one side and group two on the other.

Facilitate both sides of the discussion and then put the motion of giving Alain Baxter his medal back to the vote.

Pull out key points from the discussions and reinforce that there are 4000 drugs banned by the International Olympic Committee (IOC) who set National Standards.

'Drugs in Sports' news story

DRUGS AT THE 2002 WINTER OLYMPICS

British skier Alain Baxter tested positive in Salt Lake 2002 for methamphetamine, an addictive stimulant that affects the central nervous system.

Methamphetamine is a Class B controlled drug and is a synthetic substance closely related to the stimulant drug amphetamine. Baxter was stripped of his Bronze Olympic medal, despite protesting that he was innocent of the charges.

Later it emerged that Alain had taken a banned drug by mistake (in a nasal inhaler). He was cleared of cheating and deliberate use of illegal pharmaceuticals.

'The ban's been lifted, they've accepted it was a genuine mistake, my name's been cleared and I can work from there,' Alain said. 'That's the most important thing.'

His medal, that bronze acknowledgement of achievement, was not returned.

(*Source*: www.news.bbc.co.uk and www.sport.guardian.co.uk)

WALK ON BY?

If the young people you work with hate role-play, adapt this and facilitate it as a discussion.

Aim

To explore helping others and what to do in a drug-related emergency, including basic first aid. The activity also explores assumptions and the ethics around the decision to help or not.

You will need

- Copies of the 'Walk On By?' scenarios
- Large sheets of paper
- Marker pens

How to do it

Divide the young people into small groups and hand each group a 'Walk On By?' scenario, paper and markers. Explain that they have 20 minutes to devise a short role-play from the snapshot given that shows their response.

After all the performances, facilitate a discussion that considers the following:

1. What informed the decision to stop or not stop and help?
2. What were the factors that helped them decide, for example age or gender?
3. Did people assume that the person asking for help was drunk/drugged?

Ask if different decisions would be made if it was known that the person requiring help was suffering an asthma attack or about to slip into a diabetic coma. Suggest that it is often hard to tell what is wrong just by looking at someone, and assumptions made might be wrong.

Tell the young people that in France there is a 'Good Samaritan' law, which makes it an offence not to help a citizen in need, unless doing so would endanger the person helping. Ask the young people if they think that a similar law should be passed where they live, and discuss responses.

Finally, ask the young people the following:

- Do you need confidence to help someone else?

- Would having specific skills make a difference? What would they be?
- What's the worst that could happen if you decide to walk on by? To you and the person you haven't helped?

Stress that young people should never walk away from a friend who has taken any kind of drug, even if they are scared of the consequences. It can be very dangerous to leave someone unattended. Suggest that sometimes it is best to call someone's parents and ask for help. An alternative might be to call for emergency medical services.

Conclude by going through some basic first aid, including the recovery position.

'Walk On By?' scenarios

SCENARIO 1

On the way home a man notices a young woman lying slumped in a pub doorway. She is moaning and coughing and asking for help.

SCENARIO 2

On the way home from the pub a man notices another man lying slumped in a shop doorway. He is moaning and coughing and asking for help.

SCENARIO 3

In a club toilet a young woman notices an older woman lying slumped in a cubicle. She is moaning and coughing and asking for help.

SCENARIO 4

On the way home a young man notices another young man lying slumped in the park. He is moaning and coughing and asking for help.

SCENARIO 5

On the way to work a young woman notices an older man lying slumped on a park bench. He is moaning and coughing and asking for help.

SCENARIO 6

On the last train home a young woman notices a man slumped in his seat. He is moaning and coughing and asking for help.

BUILDING SUPPORT CIRCLES

Aims

To explore current support networks for young people and encourage them to use them for help and support when making decisions about drugs.

You will need

- Paper
- Pens

How to do it

Demonstrate drawing a support circle by drawing a series of circles one inside the other, so that it looks like a target. Then ask the young people to draw one.

Tell them to put their name in the central circle and explain that each circle around this represents a circle of people that could offer support if they were trying to give up a drug or resist peer pressure. They should put those people emotionally closest to them nearest to the centre of the circle, moving outwards towards the edge of the circles for those least close.

Read out the questions below and then ask the young people to write the name of the person that they could approach for help in the appropriate place that best represents how close they are:

1. You have broken up with someone very close to you and are feeling very lonely, sad and upset. Instead of opening a bottle of vodka or wine, who could offer you support and the opportunity to talk through your feelings?
2. You are trying to give up smoking, as you know that it is not good for you. If you were desperate for a cigarette, who could help?
3. You are going to a party where you know there will be cocaine. You don't want to participate. Which of your friends can support you in your decision?
4. Your friends have bought some legal highs online for the weekend. They are putting pressure on you to try them out. Who can help you stand up for yourself?
5. You decide that a partner's cannabis use has got out of hand and you feel worried about the impact this is having on both your lives. Who can offer you support and good advice?

6. You are worried about your own drug/alcohol use and want support to get help. Who can you ask?

Once you have asked the questions, adapting them where necessary to make them relevant to your group, talk through the findings. Facilitate a discussion that considers support networks and the value of family and friends in times of difficulty. Make sure details of local drug and alcohol support services are available and that you understand any referral process so that you can explain it to the young people. Assure them that even if they do have problems, there is support and that it is better to face and address problems rather than ignoring them. This will not automatically result in rehab or an extensive detox programme that can only be facilitated by professionals.

REVIEW TIPS

BE SAFE

This can be done individually or as part of a group.

Aim

To consider a range of safety issues and develop strategies to stay safe.

You will need

- Blank A6 pieces of card with different drug concerns on
- A3 coloured card
- Markers
- Sticky tack

How to do it

Before the session, make up the A6 cards by writing one drug concern on each. These should reflect general concerns, as well as those particular to the young people you are working with. Examples could be:

- using medication prescribed for someone else
- selling illegal drugs
- buying drugs online
- giving up
- being assertive
- mixing drugs.

Outline the session to the young people and ask them to choose a partner to work with. Place the cards face down and invite each pair to come and choose a card. Ask the young people not to share what is on their cards for the moment.

Working in their pairs, ask the young people to discuss the drug concern outlined on their card and come up with five safety issues and strategies they have learnt about it. Once they have their ideas, invite them to write them up onto the A3 coloured card.

Invite each couple to bring up their drug safety sheets and share them with the other young people, before sticking them up on the wall. Encourage comments, questions and discussions and then leave the sheets on display for future reference.

DRUGS BAG

This review technique enables young people to share what they have learnt and identify gaps for further work.

Aim

To facilitate peer learning and identify areas that will need additional work.

You will need

- Post-it notes
- Pens
- A small cloth drawstring bag

How to do it

Invite the young people to sit in a circle so that everyone can be seen and heard within the group. Hand everyone a Post-it note and a pen and ask them to write a question in the middle of the paper about drugs that they know the answer to; for example, 'What class drug is heroin?' or 'Is cocaine a stimulant or a depressant drug?' Once they have written down their question, ask the young people to fold their paper and not show anyone else.

Then pass the bag around the circle and ask each group member to put his or her slip into the bag. When all the slips have been collected, give the bag a good shake to mix the questions up. Stress that this game is not a chance to show off or make other members of the group feel stupid if they do not know the answer. It is an opportunity to learn from each other.

Now pass the bag around the circle, inviting young people to take it in turns to take a slip out of it, answer if they can and then pass the bag on. If the young person doesn't know the answer, another member of the group can answer. If no one knows then the author of the question can answer. If there are any answers given that the group is not sure about or if anyone wants to challenge an answer then facilitate this. Agree with the group any areas that they feel that they would like more information about for future sessions.

THREE THINGS

Aim

To review learning, share knowledge and challenge misinformation.

You will need

- Nothing

How to do it

Invite the young people to sit in a circle.

Then explain that each person is going to share three things about drugs that they know are correct. They will then share three things that they would like to learn more about in future. For example:

TRUE

1. In the UK heroin is a Class A drug.

2. Coffee contains caffeine.
3. Herbal remedies can be dangerous if mixed with some prescription drugs.

THINGS I WANT TO KNOW MORE ABOUT

1. The dangers of buying drugs on the internet.
2. The drug laws in different states.
3. How having a drugs conviction could affect my life.

Use the statements made as discussion points and the learning review as a needs analysis for future sessions.

ADDITIONAL SUPPORT

These websites contain information that can be useful for updating legislation and knowledge. However, the author can take no responsibility for the contents and the views expressed are not necessarily shared or endorsed.

Girls Health
www.girlshealth.gov
This US site promotes health for young women and contains information and resources.

Alcohol Concern
www.alcoholconcern.org.uk
Alcohol Concern is the national UK agency on alcohol misuse. The site contains a range of information including fact sheets.

Drugs Students Survival Guide
www.nistudentsdrugs.info/defaulttrue.asp
This site is aimed at students and gives information on drugs, drugs use, the law, health and emergencies.

DrugScope
www.drugscope.org.uk
Information on alcohol and legal and illegal drugs, the law, articles about drug issues and an encyclopaedia of drugs.

National Alcohol Campaign (Australia)
www.alcohol.gov.au

National Health and Medical Research Council (NHMRC)
www.nhmrc.gov.au

Information including safe drinking guidelines and units.

National Institute on Alcohol Abuse and Alcoholism
www.niaaa.nih.gov

American website that offers information and research.

National Substance Abuse Index
www.nationalsubstanceabuseindex.org

USA website that gives information about the Controlled Substances Act (1970) and the classification of drugs.

NHS Live Well
www.nhs.uk/livewell

UK NHS site that offers information and practical advice on a wide range of health issues, including drugs.

Re-Solv

www.re-solv.org

Re-Solv is the only national UK charity solely dedicated to the prevention of solvent and volatile substance abuse (VSA).

Talk to Frank

www.talktofrank.com

UK site mainly for young people but useful for parents/carers and professionals too. Includes alphabetical listing of drugs and their slang names.

Wotz da Factz

www.wotzdafactz.co.uk

Information on a wide range of drug-related topics, including school exclusion and drug-using parents.